WILD ANIMAL BABIES

ZEBRA FOALS

NOAH RICCARDI

PowerKiDS press

Published in 2027 by The Rosen Publishing Group, Inc.
2544 Clinton Street, Buffalo, NY 14224

First Edition

Book Design: Marley Richmond

Photo Credits: Cover, p. 1 slowmotiongli/Shutterstock.com; p. 5 EcoPrint/Shutterstock.com; p. 7 Denis Lapaev/Shutterstock.com; p. 9 Huang Jenhung/Shutterstock.com; p. 11 Karianne Borud/Shutterstock.com; p. 13 Gudkov Andrey/Shutterstock.com; p. 15 Greg Schulz Photography/Shutterstock.com; p. 17 Rahul Misra Wildlifer/Shutterstock.com; p. 19 Danita Delimont/Shutterstock.com; p. 21 Susan Rogers/Shutterstock.com.

Cataloging-in-Publication Data
Names: Riccardi, Noah.
Title: Zebra foals / Noah Riccardi.
Description: Buffalo, New York : PowerKids Press, 2027. | Series: Wild animal babies | Includes glossary and index.
Identifiers: ISBN 9781538295540 (pbk.) | ISBN 9781538295557 (library bound) | ISBN 9781538295564 (ebook)
Subjects: LCSH: Zebra--Infancy--Juvenile literature. | Foals--Juvenile literature.
Classification: LCC QL737.U62 R533 2027 | DDC 599.66571392--dc23

Manufactured in China

CPSIA Compliance Information: Batch #QS27PK. For Further Information contact Rosen Publishing, at 1-800-237-9932.

CONTENTS

All About Zebras

Zebras are **mammals** that live in **herds**. Zebras are related to horses. They are known for their black-and-white stripes. Zebras live in the **savannas** of Africa. A baby zebra is called a foal.

A Foal Is Born

A zebra mother gives birth to one foal at a time. At birth, a foal weighs around 70 pounds (32 kg). It already has stripes. But its stripes are brown and white.

Zebra foals start moving soon after they are born. They can stand up in just a few minutes. About one hour after birth, zebra foals are able to run.

Foal and Mother

A newborn foal lives with just its mother for a few days or weeks. During this time, the foal learns its mother's scent, voice, and stripes. That way, it can find her later when they join the herd.

The Herd

Wild zebras live in herds that travel together. Zebra herds can be huge. Some can have hundreds or even thousands of zebras. Joining a herd helps young zebras stay safe.

Zebras have many **predators**. These include lions, hyenas, and cheetahs. By moving in herds, zebras protect one another. They can watch for and run from danger.

Family Ties

While in the herd, a foal **nurses** from its mother. It also eats grass. Even though zebras live in herds, a mother will nurse only her own foal.

Zebras nurse until around one year old. After that, they live by **grazing**. After they are **weaned**, foals stay with their mother for a few years. They continue to grow.

Growing Old

As foals grow, their stripes darken. They turn fully black by one and a half years old. By three years old, foals can live on their own. Some stay with their herds. Others leave to join new herds.

GLOSSARY

grazing: Eating grasses.

herds: Groups of zebras.

mammals: Animals that have hair or fur and that feed milk to their babies.

nurses: Drinks milk from the body of the mother.

predators: Animals that hunt other animals for food.

savannas: Dry, flat areas with grasses and few trees.

weaned: Not needing to nurse for food anymore.

FOR MORE INFORMATION

BOOKS

Hansen, Grace. *Kenya Safari*. Minneapolis, MN: Abdo Publishing, 2025.

Schuh, Mari. *Animals of the African Savanna*. North Mankato, MN: Capstone Publishing, 2022.

WEBSITES

National Geographic Kids: Zebra
kids.nationalgeographic.com/animals/mammals/facts/zebra
Learn more about zebras at this website.

PBS LearningMedia: Zoo Safari
thinktv.pbslearningmedia.org/resource/evscps.sci.life.safari/zoo-safari/
Watch a video about savanna animals at a zoo.

INDEX